Lisa A. Durham
Dawn Hafner
Dolores Lawrence

Best Practices for ESOP-401(k) Combinations

Second Edition

Updated by Dolores Lawrence

The National Center for Employee Ownership
Visit **www.nceo.org** for more on employee ownership

Best Practices for ESOP-401(k) Combinations, 2nd Ed.

Lisa A. Durham, Dawn Hafner, and Dolores Lawrence

Book design by Scott Rodrick

ISBN: 978-1-954990-54-8

The National Center for Employee Ownership
Phone: (510) 208-1300
Website: www.nceo.org

Contents

Introduction

ROUGHLY 90% OF COMPANIES with an employee stock ownership plan (ESOP) either sponsor a separate 401(k) plan or combine ESOP and 401(k) components under the umbrella of a single plan arrangement known as a KSOP. The 401(k) plan, or 401(k) component of a KSOP, offers employees the ability to contribute toward their retirement savings. The combination of plans offers employees the ability to diversify their retirement savings investments through the 401(k) arrangement while enjoying the benefits of ownership through the ESOP. The 401(k) arrangement offers employees the ability to contribute to their retirement savings and to direct the investment of those savings. Most ESOP companies offer a 401(k) arrangement because of the diversification opportunity it provides, because the arrangement is highly desirable for attracting and retaining good employees, or to supplement the retirement income provided by the ESOP.

ESOPs and 401(k) plans are governed by the same rules that pertain to qualified plans in general, including the rules for eligibility, entry, vesting, and contribution limits. Both are subject to required participant disclosure requirements. Both have regulatory reporting requirements, including an annual Form 5500 filed with the U.S. Department of Labor (DOL) and a Form 8955-SSA filed with the

Internal Revenue Service (IRS). Both require fiduciary oversight by a plan administrator and a trustee. Beyond the basic qualified plan requirements, the designs and operations of these plans are anything but cookie-cutter. Plan designs can vary significantly. While some ESOP and 401(k) plans are operated and administered in a parallel manner, many plan designs call for integrated features. In particular, it is becoming more common, for example, to see employer matching contributions funded in an ESOP, while the related employee salary deferral contributions are funded in the 401(k) plan.

This book discusses design options, best practices for the smooth operation of multiple plans, and the challenges of clearly communicating how the plans provide benefits.

The original version of this book, released in 2013, was authored by Lisa A. Durham, Dawn Hafner, and Dolores Lawrence. The second edition (2025) was updated by Dolores Lawrence.

CHAPTER 1

Key Differences Between ESOPs and 401(k) Plans

Eligibility and Entry

While some companies design their plans to provide uniform eligibility conditions, the typical 401(k) plan offers either immediate eligibility or eligibility after completion of one to six months of service. Some 401(k) plans, however, do require a longer service period before plan entry, particularly where employee turnover is high or the plan is considered top-heavy (see below under "Top-Heavy Testing"). On the other hand, the typical ESOP sponsored by a private company requires one full year of service with the plan sponsor (generally, 1,000 hours worked in a 12-month eligibility period). Frequently, the ESOP also has a requirement that an employee be aged 21 to join the plan. The typical ESOP sponsored by a private company provides for semiannual entry dates. The conservative service and entry requirements are designed with two purposes in mind:

1. Ensure that the ESOP benefits long-term employees who contribute to the company's success.

2. Manage the growth of the ESOP repurchase obligation. Every share that is allocated to a participant must eventually be converted to cash when there is a distribution event.

Contributions and Accrual Conditions

Certainly, there are many variations on contribution levels, allocation methods, and accrual requirements. The typical ESOP is designed to reward those who stay with the company, providing an annual allocation of contributions for those who work 1,000 or more hours of service in a plan year and who are still employed on the last day of the plan year. Usually, the ESOP contributions are allocated to participants pro rata based on their eligible compensation. In contrast, the typical 401(k) plan is designed to encourage employees to make salary deferral contributions. The savings incentive is the matching contribution, often made each pay period.

However, companies considering a new ESOP design weigh all the options and often review many designs before making a decision. The options may include an allocation of points based on compensation and service, or perhaps matching or safe harbor contributions funded in the ESOP.

Distributions

The typical ESOP participant waits several years before benefit payments commence after employment termination, and payments are frequently made in installments. On the other hand, 401(k) plans usually provide for immediate and full payment after termination.

As discussed below, the differences described above may influence a company's decision to offer ESOP and 401(k) plans as paired plans versus combining the benefits of both into one plan (a KSOP).

CHAPTER 2

Important Considerations for the Company Sponsoring Both Plans

Employer Contribution Deduction Limits

A company's deduction limits are based on eligible participant compensation paid during a company's fiscal year, and the deduction limits apply to the company's combined plans. For an S corporation, the deduction limit is 25% of eligible compensation. The same limit applies to a C corporation if its ESOP is not leveraged. To the extent the ESOP is leveraged, the C corporation deduction limit is 25% of eligible compensation to the extent the contribution is used to pay loan principal, plus an unlimited deduction for contributions used to pay loan interest. Additionally, under certain circumstances, another 25% of compensation could be directed toward matching or other contributions that are not used to repay ESOP debt.

Watch Out for Different Plan Years

The calculation of maximum deductible contributions becomes more complicated when the ESOP plan year and 401(k) plan year do not match. The accountants and/or third-party administrators (TPAs) for the plans need to ensure that the deduction limit is correctly calculated based on the company's fiscal year and that contributions to both plans are considered.

Annual Addition Limits

Section 415 of the Internal Revenue Code (the "Code") dictates the maximum amount of contributions and forfeitures that can be allocated to an individual's defined contribution plan accounts during a "limitation year." Most plans define the limitation year as the plan year. This means that an individual's salary deferral contributions plus employer contributions plus an individual's share of forfeitures cannot exceed the Section 415 limit ($70,000 for plan years ending in 2025; this amount is indexed for inflation). *This limit can be exceeded only if the excess consists of an individual's catch-up deferrals (if the participant is aged 50 or older).*

If a company is using a different TPA for each plan, it is important to have one TPA assigned the responsibility of calculating the combined Section 415 annual additions for each participant in a limitation year and determining the appropriate corrections if any participant's allocations exceed the annual limit. If a company sponsors more than one plan, the plans should include coordinating language that dictates in which plan the Section 415 excess contributions are corrected.

What if a company sponsors a 401(k) plan with a calendar limitation year, plus an ESOP with a limitation year ending each September 30? In that situation, two Section 415 calculations would be needed annually to capture the total allocations to an individual's accounts in each limitation year! If two plans have different plan years, the plan sponsor should consider drafting the plans to have the same "limitation year" so that only one annual Section 415 calculation is needed.

What if an individual participant's contributions in the company's ESOP and 401(k) plans exceed the applicable limit? Both plan documents should define how corrections are made, and those terms should match across plans. The ESOP may provide that an individual's excess annual additions are corrected in the ESOP through reallocating the excess to other eligible ESOP participants. However, the documents may provide for correction to be made in the company's 401(k) plan in the manner outlined in the Internal Revenue Service's Employee Plans Compliance Resolution System (EPCRS). EPCRS procedures outline the following order for correction:

- Distribute unmatched voluntary after-tax contributions, if any.
- Distribute unmatched salary deferral contributions.
- Distribute matched voluntary after-tax contributions, if any, and forfeit the related match.
- Distribute matched salary deferrals and forfeit the related match.

The amounts distributed are adjusted for earnings. A 401(k) TPA's software *may* be able to run the correction calculations, though some 401(k) software programs are not designed to run them. That can mean that manual calculations are required. Some 401(k) TPAs that work primarily on standalone 401(k) plans may have limited experience making these corrections. For 401(k) plans subject to ADP/ACP nondiscrimination testing, the tests should be rerun after the corrections are made. The testing results may be different from any tests that were run before the corrections were made, adding a new headache for the TPA to address.

For companies that sponsor both plans and that make generous contributions to these plans, dealing with Section 415 excess annual additions may become an annual event. In those cases, it helps if the company's plan administrator understands how the excess annual additions occurred and investigates ways to keep this from being a yearly occurrence. Changes in plan design or funding decisions could make a difference. Perhaps caps on salary deferral contributions would help, or perhaps a hard decision to reduce employer contributions to the company's 401(k) plan is needed. ESOP changes could also be made. For a plan making a new leveraged stock acquisition, consideration should be given to using a long-term loan (for example, 40 years or more) with a right of prepayment. Having such a loan might help decrease unusually high benefit levels in the ESOP. A plan sponsor could also decide to distribute shares (subject to repurchase by the company) instead of cash if that might reduce the funding of contributions that ESOP needs to pay benefits. This might be done to reduce unusually high benefit levels to reasonable levels.

Top-Heavy Testing

In general (without getting into the details of the calculations), a company's defined contribution plans are top-heavy if, on an aggregated basis, the accounts of "key employees" make up 60% or more of combined plan accounts. If a company's plans are top-heavy, minimum employer contributions may be due to certain participants. If a company has different TPAs for each of its defined contribution plans, one TPA should be assigned the responsibility of completing the annual top-heavy calculation and determining whether the combined plans are top-heavy. If a company's plans are top-heavy, the plan documents should include coordinating language that specifies which of the plans will satisfy any top-heavy funding requirements. A participant is eligible for a top-heavy contribution as soon as they are eligible to make deferrals, so care should be exercised when the 401(k) plan has an earlier entry date than the ESOP.

"Highly Compensated Employee" Definition

On an annual basis, those who are "highly compensated employees" (HCEs) must be identified so that the TPA can run the nondiscrimination tests that apply to a plan, be that an ESOP, 401(k), or other plan. Part 1 of the HCE definition includes individuals who own or owned more than 5% of the company or an affiliate on any day in the current or prior year (plus those who are more-than-5% owners through family attribution). Part 2 includes those who earned over a certain amount in the prior (lookback) year. For a plan year ending on December 31, 2025, HCEs include those who earned more than $155,000 in calendar year 2024. However, it is possible to limit the number of HCEs included in part 2 by using what is called the "top-paid group election." That limitation can prove useful in a company that has a significant number of HCEs. If a company sponsors more than one plan and makes the top-paid group election for one plan, it needs to make that election for all plans it sponsors. TPAs should compare records to ensure their HCE groups match for each plan.

Multiple Plan Coordination

The above discussion highlights the importance of making sure plan providers are aware that a company sponsors more than one plan. It is critical for a company to assign responsibility for contribution deduction calculations and combined testing. Usually, the ESOP TPA performs the combined testing. The ESOP TPA should receive copies of all plan documents, even if not providing services for a company's 401(k) plan. Both the ESOP TPA and the company's ERISA (Employee Retirement Income Security Act of 1974) counsel for the ESOP can and should review both plans to ensure that they contain coordinating top-heavy, Section 415, and other language.

If a company sponsors a KSOP and the recordkeeping for the ESOP component and the 401(k) component of the plan are maintained separately, the ESOP TPA will generally be responsible for preparation of the annual Form 5500 and Form 8955-SSA for the KSOP. To prepare these returns, data will need to be provided by the 401(k) TPA.

All too often, there are mistakes made when a company sponsors both an ESOP and a 401(k) plan and uses different TPAs for each plan's compliance testing. There are differences in who is reported as highly compensated or as a key employee. It is extremely important that the company's plan administrator provide the same key metrics to each TPA: outside owners and their ownership percentages, identification of family members of these owners if they are also employees, and identification of corporate officers.

Fiduciary Responsibility

The plan sponsor is responsible for selecting and monitoring the plan providers it hires, including reviewing and determining that written service agreements are compliant with ERISA and provide sufficient details of the provider's duties. The plan sponsor is also responsible for determining what compensation is being paid to plan providers, both direct and indirect, and determining that the compensation paid is reasonable.

Vendor Fee Disclosures

Under the terms of ERISA Section 408(b)(2), "covered service providers" (CSPs) must disclose to plan fiduciaries what direct and indirect compensation they receive and the services they provide for that compensation. A CSP is a provider that reasonably expects to receive direct and indirect compensation exceeding $1,000 over the term of a contract. A TPA paid solely by the plan sponsor (an arrangement that is typical for ESOPs) is generally not a CSP. However, a 401(k) plan, KSOP, or ESOP that permits any self-direction of investment may have CSPs that are required to provide fee disclosures to plan sponsors. For more information on these disclosure rules, see appendix A to this book. If a plan sponsor is unsure whether a TPA or other service provider is a CSP, it is best to ask the provider to (1) provide a written disclosure statement that complies with the requirements of ERISA Section 408(b)(2) or (2) provide a written statement indicating why the provider is not a CSP.

Participant Fee Disclosures

Under the terms of ERISA Section 404(a)(5), plan participants are entitled to receive annual and quarterly fee disclosure statements if any accounts in a plan permit self-directed investment. The fee disclosure requirements of the typical 401(k) plan are provided by the TPA or investment platform provider for the plan. It is important to note that the fee disclosures may apply to an ESOP if any ESOP accounts are subject to self-directed investment. This would include ESOPs that permit eligible participants to diversify a portion of their employer stock accounts and invest the proceeds in three or more diversified investment options that are provided *in the ESOP.* This would also include ESOPs that segregate the accounts of terminated participants into cash or other non-employer stock investments and then permit participants to self-direct the investment of segregated funds.

What about an ESOP whose provisions state that diversification elections are handled solely through liquidation of employer stock in the ESOP and transfer of proceeds to a separate 401(k) plan? Because of the transfer limitation, it can be argued that the ESOP employer stock becomes a "designated investment alternative" because a diversification-eligible participant must choose between staying invested in stock or investing in the options provided in the 401(k) plan. In this case, a Section 404(a)(5)-compliant fee disclosure notice should be provided annually to diversification-eligible participants along with their diversification election forms. This creates some disclosure challenges, including the need to derive historical rate-of-return data for the employer stock and compare that rate-of-return information to an appropriate benchmark. The benchmark could be the Russell 3000, for example, or any other benchmark that company management deems appropriate.

While the participant fee disclosure rules clearly apply to the participant-directed 401(k) component of a KSOP plan, DOL Field Assistance Bulletin 2012-2, Question and Answer 1, taken literally, may cause consternation for some KSOP sponsors. Question and Answer 1 deal with a plan that provides a combination of both participant-directed investment and trustee-directed investment. Such a plan is a "covered individual account plan" that is subject to the participant fee disclosure rules as a whole. That generally means the annual participant fee disclosure statement given to participants should include the 401(k)-related disclosures that are required, including the applicable investment disclosures for participant-directed accounts, *plus* disclosures concerning any fees or expenses that may be deducted from ESOP accounts that are subject to trustee-directed investment. To meet this requirement, an ESOP addendum may need to be attached to any disclosure statement that is prepared for the 401(k) component of the plan.

See appendix B to this book for additional information.

CHAPTER 3

General Design Options

Side-by-Side Plans—Minimal Integration of Features

For most companies that sponsor two or more plans, the plans are operated independently of each other, except for the need to aggregate the plans when calculating deduction limits or completing top-heavy and annual addition tests. While it may make administrative sense (and minimize errors) if both plans have the same definition of compensation, that is not a requirement. The plans typically have different requirements for eligibility, plan entry, contribution sources, eligibility to share in contributions, vesting, and so forth.

Match in the ESOP

A number of ESOPs provide for either a required match or a discretionary match to be funded in the ESOP. Typically, ESOPs with a match provision provide that the match is discretionary, as determined annually by the board of directors. The ESOP may state that matching contributions can be made in cash or employer stock. The ESOP may state that the plan sponsor will determine annually whether a discretionary match will be funded in the ESOP or in the 401(k) plan. Most ESOPs that include matching provisions provide for an annual match, perhaps allocated only to those employed on the last day of the plan year who also completed 1,000 hours of service in the plan year. Few ESOPs provide for a match that is calculated and funded each pay period, though there is no prohibition against doing so.

If a match will be used to pay ESOP debt with a resultant share release, it is helpful if the plan document states whether the match is measured based on dollars contributed or the fair value of shares released due to the match. In addition, expect more questions from participants when their match is used to pay debt.

> ***Example.*** Mary contributes $12,000 in salary deferrals to ABC Company's 401(k) plan. The company states that an annual matching contribution equal to 10% of salary deferrals will be funded in the ESOP. Mary's anticipated match is $1,200. The match is used to pay principal and interest on ESOP debt. After a principal-plus-interest share release is calculated, the ESOP TPA determines that 50 shares are released from suspense due to Mary's match. Based on the year-end appraisal report, each share has a fair value of $20. So Mary's ESOP match account is credited with 50 shares of employer stock with a fair value of $1,000.

In considering a match feature for the ESOP, it is necessary to consider the written provisions of both plans, ESOP and 401(k). What if a company's 401(k) plan has immediate eligibility and entry at date of hire for all purposes for employees who are 18 years of age, while the ESOP requires employees to attain the age of 21 and complete one year of service (1,000 hours in a 12-month computation period)? What if both plans have a discretionary match provision, but the 401(k) plan provides for vesting over five years, and the ESOP provides for vesting over six years? All of these provisions need to be considered together before a match provision can be incorporated into an ESOP document.

If an ESOP includes a match feature, the TPA must be prepared to timely prepare each year's actual contribution percentage (ACP) test and provide corrective action for a failed test. In general, without going into the nuts and bolts of the test, the ACP test compares the average match contribution rate of HCEs to the average match rate of non-highly compensated participants. If the average match rate for the

HCE group exceeds the average match rate for other participants by more than a certain formula, refunds or forfeitures of some matching contributions will be required.

If a plan sponsor is using different TPAs for its 401(k) plan and ESOP, it is advisable to review the actual deferral percentage (ADP) test and the ACP test together to ensure the same employees in each test have been identified as HCEs.

Safe Harbor Contributions in the ESOP

Companies may wish to avoid ADP/ACP testing by adopting a "safe harbor 401(k)" provision. In a safe harbor plan, employer contributions are required and are 100% vested. There *cannot* be accrual conditions for sharing in safe harbor contributions, like a requirement that a participant work 1,000 hours in a plan year or be employed on the last day of the plan year. In addition, advance written notices must be given to participants before they become eligible to participate and then annually at least 30 days and no more than 90 days before the beginning of each plan year.

While safe harbor contributions are usually funded in a company's 401(k) plan, they can instead be funded in the ESOP. Safe harbor notices for participants should specify which plan is receiving safe harbor employer contributions.

Safe harbor formulas that result in 100% vested contributions include the following:

- Three percent (or greater) of each participant's compensation, as defined by the plan; it can be limited to just non-highly compensated employees.
- A basic match—dollar-for-dollar on the first 3% of compensation contributed by a participant as a salary deferral, plus 50% of the next 2% of compensation contributed. For a participant deferring 5% or more of their compensation, the maximum match is 4% of compensation.

- An enhanced match—100% of the first 4% contributed by a participant as a salary deferral (or similar formula, with some limitations).

As an alternative, a company could provide for a qualified automatic contribution arrangement (QACA). The advantage of this arrangement is that contributions do not have to be fully vested until completion of two years of vesting service. Under a QACA arrangement, safe harbor contributions are paired with automatic enrollment in the company's 401(k) plan. Under the QACA arrangement, employer contribution options include:

- Three percent (or greater) of each participant's compensation, as defined by the plan; it can be limited to just non-highly compensated employees.
- A basic match—dollar-for-dollar on the first 1% of compensation deferred, plus 50% of the next 5% of compensation deferred by a participant. For a participant deferring 6% or more of their compensation, the maximum match is 3.5% of compensation.
- An enhanced match—a mathematical equivalent of the basic match, with limitations.

The plan must provide automatic enrollment of those who fail to affirmatively complete a salary deferral election form. Automatic enrollment can start at a default rate of 3% or more of a participant's compensation, and must escalate annually by 1% each year until it reaches at least 6% but not more than 10% of pay. An easy alternative is to simply set the default rate at 6% from the outset.

What Is the Downside to Funding Safe Harbor Contributions in the ESOP?

- Because there are no accrual conditions for sharing in safe harbor contributions and they are generally vested at all times, such contributions can accelerate a company's repurchase obligation.

- In recordkeeping, safe harbor contributions (and earnings) must be entered as a separate contribution source because there are statutory distribution restrictions that apply. Such contributions are not eligible for in-service withdrawal before termination of employment or attainment of age 59½. That may play havoc with diversification rights if the ESOP provides that diversified amounts may be distributed to participants.
- What if a safe harbor contribution of 3% of pay is equal to $1,000, but it is used to pay down ESOP debt that releases shares worth $900? Here, the IRS guidance is not totally clear, and there are differences of opinion among attorneys who work with ESOPs. At one ESOP Association conference in Washington, DC, a panel of IRS experts was asked whether a safe harbor contribution needed to be made whole; that is, must an ESOP participant be allocated shares with a value that is at least equal to their safe harbor contribution in dollars? The panel members informally answered that they believed the contribution should be made whole, though their opinions cannot be construed as formal guidance. Therefore, the plan sponsor who wishes to make safe harbor contributions in an ESOP is advised to have the ESOP document clearly indicate whether "make whole" rules apply.

If safe harbor contributions are to be made in the ESOP and the ESOP and 401(k) have different TPAs, responsibility must be delegated for the completion and delivery of participant safe harbor notices. Both the company's 401(k) plan document and ESOP document must state that safe harbor contributions will be funded in the ESOP. If the plan is a KSOP, it is not necessary to state whether the safe harbor contribution is made to the ESOP component or the 401(k) component, only that the safe harbor will be made to the KSOP.

As with matching contributions (discussed above), it is necessary to consider each plan's eligibility and entry provisions. What if, for example, participants are immediately eligible to make salary deferrals in the 401(k) plan, but must attain the age of 21 and complete one year of service to be eligible in the ESOP? If safe harbor contributions are allocated only to those who are ESOP-eligible, it may be necessary to prepare an annual ADP test that includes only those 401(k) participants who are not ESOP-eligible. If this group consists solely of non-highly compensated employees, the test will automatically pass.

Transfers Between Plans: Beware of the Landmines

ESOP provisions sometimes call for transfers from the ESOP to the company's 401(k) plan, or from the 401(k) plan to the ESOP. Samples of transfer provisions include:

- *Diversification.* In an ESOP sponsored by a private company, a participant who attains the age of 55 and completes 10 years of plan participation will be given the right to diversify a portion of their ESOP shares. The ESOP specifies what happens when a participant diversifies. The proceeds may be distributed to the participant, or the participant might be able to elect a transfer to the company's 401(k) plan or a rollover to an IRA. Alternatively, the plan could dictate that diversification proceeds transfer to the company's 401(k) plan. With a plan-to-plan transfer, the mechanics are important. The 401(k) plan must permit transfer accounts. An ESOP transfer account needs to be established in the 401(k) plan recordkeeping system, and the transferred amounts need to be deposited to this account, not to a rollover account. The ESOP transfer account would typically be subject to withdrawal restrictions. Most 401(k) plans permit withdrawal from rollover accounts at any time. Thus, they are not the appropriate accounts for receiving diversification proceeds.
- *Reshuffling (sometimes referred to as segregation of terminated participant accounts).* An ESOP plan document may provide for the transfer of employer stock out of terminated participant accounts. Typically, the cash in the ESOP accounts of active participants is

used to acquire the shares, and the terminated participants' shares are replaced with cash transferred from the accounts of active participants. The ESOP typically provides that the segregated funds be invested appropriately within the ESOP. There needs to be a return on investment. However, the plan sponsor might prefer to see segregated funds transferred to the company's 401(k) plan. Again, the devil is in the details—the mechanics for transfer and communications between plan service providers. Not all 401(k) recordkeepers will permit these transfers, especially if the transferred amounts are partially vested. The 401(k) plan needs to permit transfer accounts, and the recordkeeper needs to be willing to accommodate the transfers and track the transferred amounts appropriately in the recordkeeping system. See the paragraph on diversification transfers immediately above for additional considerations on mechanics. What if the transferred amounts are partially vested? Will the nonvested portion of the accounts stay in the 401(k) plan or be transferred back to the ESOP when there is a forfeiture event? It is important to work out the details before implementing transfers.

- *Voluntary transfers.* While it is not a frequent occurrence, some plans will sometimes provide a transfer opportunity to 401(k) participants. An offering memorandum may tell 401(k) participants that they may elect to transfer all or a portion of their 401(k) account to the ESOP, where it will be used to acquire shares. Such transfers require assistance from ERISA counsel to properly administer the offering and address securities registration rules.

SECURE Legislation and Plan Design

The original SECURE Act was enacted in December 2019. SECURE 2.0 was enacted in 2022. The new provisions included a myriad of required and optional provisions with staggered effective dates. Those included changes in minimum distribution rules, salary deferral catch-up contributions, and much more. Many changes are optional, such as matching contributions on student loan repayments and emergency savings accounts. Roth accounts are no longer subject to required minimum distributions (RMDs). Many of the optional provisions may be considered for 401(k) plans but are unlikely to be a good fit for ESOPs or may not apply to ESOPs at all.

Some provisions that may result in a headache for the ESOP sponsor and/or TPA:

- *Super catch-up contributions.* Starting in 2025, a 401(k) plan may permit higher catch-up salary deferrals for participants aged 60 to 63. For 2025, the normal age 50 catch-up deferral limit is $7,500. The super catch-up limit is $11,250. It will be important for plan sponsors to identify the catch-up amounts for their TPAs so that Section 415 annual additions can be calculated. (See separate discussion below on annual additions.)
- *Roth catch-up contributions.* Beginning in 2026, certain high-paid participants can make catch-up contributions only if they are Roth deferrals. "Highly paid" participants are defined by reference to their FICA wages in the prior year. For example, in 2026, a highly paid participant is 50 years old or older and had FICA wages over $145,000 in the previous calendar year. How does that affect an ESOP? Suppose Joe Participant's contributions from all plans (annual additions) exceed the Section 415 limit in 2026. Joe, aged 55 and a highly paid employee, made salary deferral contributions of $20,000 in 2026. At first glance, Joe did not make any catch-up contributions from his pay. Can the ESOP TPA recharacterize a portion of his deferrals as catch-up?
- *Roth treatment for employer contributions.* SECURE 2.0 makes it possible for a company to amend plan provisions and permit participants to designate matching or nonelective contributions as Roth contributions. For Roth treatment, the contributions must be 100% vested. Participants are taxed on the contribution amounts when allocated to their accounts. Could this be implemented in

an ESOP? Technically, yes, and we do have some IRS guidance on this option. However, 401(k) and ESOP service providers must deal with understanding the mechanics, the work involved in tracking Roth accounts, and the software changes needed for recordkeeping systems. Expect slow adoption and implementation, and higher service provider fees.

KSOP Design

A company can sponsor a KSOP that includes both a 401(k) component and an ESOP component. Advantages, disadvantages, and other considerations are discussed more fully in the next chapter, "Considerations in Designing the Second Plan."

CHAPTER 4

Considerations in Designing the Second Plan

Adding an ESOP When a 401(k) Plan Already Exists

Plan Design

A company's ESOP design is likely to be quite different from its 401(k) plan design. As discussed below, this will present any number of employee communication challenges.

A best-practice approach to ESOP design starts with preparation of a summary of the company's 401(k) plan key provisions. Using the summary as a starting point, the plan sponsor, together with legal counsel, decides which provisions in the 401(k) plan should be mirrored in the ESOP and which should not.

- *Plan year.* It is advisable to have the ESOP plan year coincide with the company's fiscal year and, preferably, with the 401(k) plan year as well. However, many 401(k) plan TPAs have a strong preference for working with calendar-year plans, as it simplifies their ADP/ACP testing processes. So a plan sponsor may end up with two plans that have different plan years. See chapter 1, "Key

Differences Between ESOPs and 401(k) Plans," for a discussion of the complications created when the plans have different years.

- *Compensation definition.* It is advisable to use the same definition of compensation for the plans, so that one annual census file can be used for the administration of both plans. For example, ABC Company's 401(k) plan document defines "Compensation" as W-2 compensation. The company's ESOP document defines "Compensation" as W-2 compensation excluding fringe benefits. On audit, it is discovered that the same annual census records have been provided to the TPAs for the company's respective plans. Both include fringe benefits. The ESOP recordkeeping must now be corrected.
- *Disability definition.* Use the same definition in both plans to avoid participant confusion.
- *Highly compensated employee.* This must use the same definition in both plans.
- *Eligibility exclusions.* Generally, any eligibility exclusions should be mirrored in both plans unless there is a compelling reason not to do so. If union employees, nonresident aliens, leased employees, temporary/seasonal employees, or other employees are excluded from participation in one plan, it may be reasonable to exclude these categories of employees for both plans.
- *Vesting.* Using the same vesting schedule in each plan saves participant confusion.
- *Consent limits.* Most plans specify a limit for paying distributions without consent if a participant fails to consent to a distribution when it is offered. It may be desirable for both plans to have the same consent limit. It is a plan design decision, and they do not have to match. The maximum "force out" distribution limit for small balances is $7,000 (it was $5,000 before 2024).

Beyond these considerations, it is likely that ESOP provisions will not match those in the 401(k) plan. However, there is no one design that fits the needs of each company. Table 4-1 presents a sample result from a theoretical plan design discussion, solely as a means of illustrating some of the design points that merit discussion. In this example, design differences stemmed primarily from the plan sponsor's desire to reward those who stay with the company and the plan sponsor's concerns about controlling the growth of its repurchase obligation. In particular, distributions following termination of employment are postponed so that the company can do cash flow planning for future payouts.

Table 4-1. Sample key plan provisions for a hypothetical company

Provision	401(k)	ESOP
Compensation	W-2 definition	W-2 definition; for contribution accrual purposes, recognize compensation from entry date forward
Eligibility	Age 21, no service requirement	Age 21, completion of one year of service
Entry	First day in which age requirement is met	Semiannual entry dates
Contribution accrual conditions	No conditions for sharing in match; 1,000 hours required for profit sharing	Completion of 1,000 hours in plan year, and employed last day of plan year; exceptions for death, disability, retirement
Contribution formula	Salary deferrals, discretionary match each pay period, discretionary profit sharing—integrated formula	Allocation to participants pro rata based on eligible compensation
Employer contribution vesting	5-year graded; recognize all service for vesting	6-year graded; recognize service for vesting beginning with the effective date of the plan
Forfeiture disposition	Pay plan expenses; remainder used to offset employer contributions	Allocate in same manner as contributions
Accelerated vesting	100% death, disability, retirement	100% death, disability, retirement

Table 4-1. Sample key plan provisions for a hypothetical company

Provision	401(k)	ESOP
Normal retirement age	65	65+ completion of 5 service years
Distribution timing	As soon as feasible after employment termination	ESOP statutory requirement only—postpone commencement of payout as long as possible
Distribution consent limit	Pay vested balance under $1,000 without consent if participant fails to elect payout	Pay vested balance under $1,000 without consent if participant fails to elect payout
In service withdrawal	Hardship, age 59½	None, except as required to meet diversification requirements
QDROs—payment to alternate payee	Pay as soon as DRO is approved	Postpone payment as permitted
Rollover contributions	Yes	No
Participant loans	Yes	No

Estimating Funding Requirements When Implementing a New ESOP

With a leveraged ESOP in particular, a company must be able to project ESOP funding requirements, including cash needed to enable the ESOP to repay its debt and cash needed for distributions and diversification elections. A new ESOP will not have immediate funding needs if it delays distributions as allowed by statute. However, plans must provide for accelerated payout if termination is due to death, disability, or retirement. While distribution funding requirements can only be estimated, it is important to consider the age of the company's workforce and the number who are at or approaching normal retirement age.

As discussed above, the company's contribution deduction limit applies to the total of all contributions it makes to its 401(k) plan and ESOP. If the company has historically funded a match in its 401(k) plan, will that continue? Or should all funding be directed to the ESOP? How will 401(k) participation be affected if a match is either eliminated or redirected into the ESOP? If the company contributes as much as possible to the ESOP, will that cause certain individuals to exceed their Section 415 annual addition limits? As discussed above, the company's contribution deduction limit applies to the total of all contributions it makes to its 401(k) plan and ESOP. If the company has historically funded a match in its 401(k) plan, will that continue? Or should all funding be directed to the ESOP? How will 401(k) participation be affected if a match is either eliminated or redirected into the ESOP? If the company contributes as much as possible to the ESOP, will that cause certain individuals to exceed their Section 415 annual addition limits? Assume an individual participant has annual compensation of $160,000 and is making annual salary deferral contributions of $23,500 in 2025. That's just over 14% of compensation. Assume a match of 100% of the first 6% of annual compensation that the employee is deferring, or $9,600 (.06 x $160,000). With an annual addition limit of $70,000 in 2025, that means this employee's allocations in the ESOP cannot exceed $36,900 ($70,000 limit - $23,500 deferral - $9,600 match), or roughly 23% of their compensation.

Therefore, it is important to run projected contribution estimates before deciding on the final provisions of a stock acquisition note. A plan sponsor should fully consider its estimated deduction limit and the possibility that large contributions could cause some participants to have excess annual additions that require correction.

> ***Example.*** ABC Company has an annual payroll of $5 million. It contributes generous matching contributions to its 401(k) plan. Included in the $5 million base is the compensation of interns and temporary employees, who are excluded from plan participation, as well as the compensation of other employees who will not stay with the company long enough to become eligible for participation in its retirement plans. In addition, many key executives have annual earnings that exceed the individual annual compensation limit,

as adjusted periodically for cost-of-living changes ($350,000 for plan years beginning in calendar year 2025). Initially, the company estimates that its deduction limit should be based on $5 million in payroll, and proceeds accordingly to have ESOP loan documents executed without first running detailed projections.

Once the total *eligible* compensation of participants is accumulated, the compensation base for the deduction limit is determined to be $3 million, not $5 million. The company must now rethink the payment terms for the ESOP acquisition loan. If the loan terms are already in effect, what does it do? Consider a loan modification agreement? Plug the funding gap with company dividends? What if the ESOP does not own 100% of shares outstanding? Outside shareholders would need to receive their share of dividends.

How Can a Company's 401(k) Plan Be Used to Meet the Needs of Its ESOP?

As briefly mentioned above, it is possible to provide initial ESOP funding (or later funding for a second-stage transaction) by permitting participants to elect to use some portion of their profit-sharing or 401(k) accounts to acquire employer stock in an ESOP. (Please note that securities law issues need to be reviewed in these designs.) Or perhaps a profit-sharing plan can be converted into an ESOP or KSOP, with a portion of existing funds used to acquire new shares of employer stock. In certain situations (primarily with ESOPs sponsored by public companies), employees may elect to have a portion of their salary deferrals used to acquire ESOP shares. The company's profit-sharing or 401(k) plan can also be used in conjunction with plan transfers due to diversification elections and segregation of terminated participant accounts.

Diversification

An ESOP holding privately held employer stock must provide participants with the right to diversify a portion of the employer stock in their accounts once they attain the age of 55 and complete 10 years of plan participation. Such a "qualified participant" is eligible to diversify up to 25% of their shares in year one of a six-year diversification window.

In years two through five, a participant may be able to diversify up to 25% of incremental new shares, and in the final and sixth year, diversify up to 50% of the shares that have ever been allocated to their account, less previously diversified shares.

There are three possible options for the disposal of the proceeds from an individual participant's diversification election: distribution to the participant, transfer to a 401(k) plan or profit-sharing plan with participant-directed investments, or creation of at least three diverse investment options within the ESOP. Many plans keep it simple by using the first option only (distribution). However, those who feel the need to keep retirement nest eggs intact until retirement or other termination of employment may prefer option two—a transfer to the company's 401(k) or other plan. This option also tends to result in fewer dollars diversified overall. The 401(k) plan must accept such transfers, and it may be necessary for the 401(k) recordkeeper to establish a separate contribution source, such as "ESOP Transfer." In the case of a KSOP, the transfer is made from the ESOP component of the plan to the 401(k) component of the plan. The third diversification option (self-directed investment funds within the ESOP trust) is generally not recommended due to administrative complexity, the associated cost of recordkeeping, and the fact that such funds would be subject to the participant fee disclosure rules of ERISA Section 404(a)(5). A transfer of diversification funds to the 401(k) plan permits participants to self-direct these funds, generally with minimal or no increased recordkeeping costs.

Segregation

Some ESOP documents provide for "reshuffling" or "segregation," which is the exchange of employer stock held in terminated participant accounts for other assets. In a typical plan with segregation language, the cash of active participants is used to acquire the shares of those who have terminated employment. This is often accomplished as a final step in the annual recordkeeping process. Once funds are "segregated," the plan sponsor has an obligation to suitably invest the segregated funds. In addressing its fiduciary obligations, a plan sponsor could consider the age of terminated participants and the timeline to distribution, among other things. The purpose of this book is *not* to get into a detailed discussion of segregation techniques and investment options. However, some plan sponsors may feel that they want to mitigate the fiduciary burden by offering some form of self-directed investment to participants with segregated accounts. While it is possible to establish participant-directed accounts within the ESOP, that option brings in a host of administrative headaches described above. Another option is to consider transferring the funds to the 401(k) plan. In a KSOP setting or a separate 401(k) plan, it might be possible to transfer the funds to the 401(k) recordkeeper that establishes segregated ESOP source accounts within its daily recordkeeping system.

Adding a 401(k) Plan When an ESOP Already Exists

What if a company adds a 401(k) as its second retirement plan? Again, there are participant communication issues to address. What if employees "assume" the 401(k) plan will come with a match? If it is a salary deferral-only plan, will employees contribute enough to make the plan a worthwhile endeavor? Is the second plan needed to attract and retain talented employees? (See the "Communication Challenges" section below.)

The same design considerations apply as in the discussion of adopting the 401(k) first and the ESOP later. No second plan should ever be designed without considering the core provisions of the first plan.

Is there a risk that an insufficient number of employees (especially those who are not highly compensated) will contribute to the 401(k) from their pay if they are already receiving generous employer-funded benefits in the ESOP? That certainly is a risk and a real possibility, depending on the level of benefits provided in the ESOP. For the company that is considering adding a 401(k), it is a good idea to perform an employee survey, asking employees on a nonbinding basis whether they would contribute to a 401(k) plan with no match, or whether they would contribute to a plan with a match. If survey results indicate that a projected ADP test would fail due to poor participation, consider the feasibility of adding a match to the company's ESOP. The match in the ESOP could either be used to pay ESOP acquisition debt or be used to purchase the shares of terminating participants. Also consider one of the safe harbor 401(k) designs that are available to companies that want a "free pass" on ADP testing. These design options are discussed in more detail in chapter 3, "General Design Options."

As a reminder, adding a 401(k) plan as a second plan may constrain funding in the ESOP since company deduction limits apply to the combined company contributions made to *both* plans. Additionally, with a 401(k) plan added, there is a greater risk that a participant's contribution and forfeiture allocations in both plans could cause an excess annual additions problem. That is, a participant's allocations in the combined plans might exceed the current Code Section 415 limit ($70,000 in 2025). Note that a participant's combined allocations can exceed the limit with no correction needed if the excess consists solely of age 50 catch-up deferrals.

Standalone Plan or KSOP?

The decision to sponsor a KSOP, versus a separate 401(k) plan and ESOP, will be made after weighing many factors. One important factor is whether one TPA will administer the entire KSOP or whether there will be separate TPAs for the ESOP and 401(k) components, but one plan document.

- *Public or private company.* The KSOP arrangement often works well for public companies, as one TPA can be engaged, and the records for the entire plan can be easily maintained in a daily recordkeeping system. The fair value of the stock and other investments can be updated daily.

- *Activity frequency.* Some private companies find it desirable to have KSOP accounts maintained on a daily recordkeeping system even if the employer stock value is updated only annually. If the company is paying cash dividends on employer stock periodically throughout the year (e.g., quarterly), such dividends can be posted to ESOP cash accounts when paid. If a company is contributing stock or paying stock dividends, the new shares are reflected in accounts at payment dates. Stock accounts can be updated to reflect shares distributed at the distribution date. Participants can check their combined balances easily; however, there may be confusion when the employer stock price is updated only once a year.
- *Degree of integration.* The KSOP document is flexible. It lends itself well to the description of a plan's integrated features. Suppose, for example, that a company wishes to make a decision annually as to the funding of matching contributions in the ESOP component or the 401(k) component. For example, the plan may state, "For each year, the Employer may contribute a matching contribution in the ESOP portion of the Plan. The matching contributions to the ESOP may be made in cash or stock. Alternatively, the Employer may contribute its matching contribution to the 401(k) portion of the Plan. To the extent that an ESOP Acquisition Loan is outstanding during the Plan year, the matching contributions, if any, will be allocated to ESOP accounts."
- *Cost.* There may be some cost savings associated with the following:
  - One plan document
  - One amendment required by legislation
  - One summary plan description
  - One Form 5500
  - One audit (if over 100 participants)
  - One summary annual report

  However, the cost savings may be minimal, particularly when there are separate custodial and/or recordkeeping functions for the 401(k) component and the ESOP component. For example, assume ABC Company sponsors a KSOP and uses XYZ Insurance Company for custodianship and daily recordkeeping of the 401(k) component. ZZZ Trust Company holds ESOP stock and other assets of the ESOP component, and ESOP recordkeeping is provided by JJJ, the TPA. Audit and recordkeeping fees for the KSOP may approximate the total costs for two separate plans.

- *Communications.* Every plan's summary plan description (SPD) should be written in a manner that is easily understood by participants. This is particularly true for KSOPs. The SPD should clearly explain the purposes of each component of the plan and its key provisions. Even with a carefully drafted SPD and other communication and enrollment materials, a KSOP can be confusing to new participants. The plan sponsor should expect questions and should be ready to describe how the plan works. If participants receive integrated statements of their accounts that include both the ESOP and 401(k) component sources, the plan sponsor should consider providing a "How to Read My Statement" guide. If participants receive separate statements for their accounts in the ESOP and 401(k) components of the KSOP, the statements should indicate that they represent just the ESOP account or just the 401(k) account of a participant. The same principle should apply to enrollment, distribution, and administrative forms.
- *Participant statements.* Often, a company will want the ESOP to stand out separately from the 401(k) to highlight the fact that it is a 100% company-funded benefit and that it is an ownership plan, not simply a retirement savings plan. Another factor in combining plans is that the ESOP statement itself often has separate features, such as shares released and loan payments. That can be confusing to the participants when combined with standard 401(k) transactions such as contributions, an employer match, and dividends invested into a menu of fund options.
- *Other administrative issues to consider.* Coordination is key, especially if separate recordkeeping systems are used for the ESOP

component and 401(k) component. As previously discussed, deduction limits and annual addition limits are determined on an aggregated basis, not a plan-by-plan or component-by-component basis. Also consider:

- *Distribution consent limits.* If the KSOP provides that participants with vested balances greater than $7,000 cannot receive a distribution without written consent, the consent threshold will apply to the entire plan and not to the separate components.
- *Lump-sum distributions and net unrealized appreciation.* If employer stock is being distributed to participants, participants may be interested in obtaining net unrealized appreciation (NUA) tax treatment. If certain conditions are met and a participant receives a lump-sum distribution from the KSOP, the participant may be able to pay ordinary income tax on the cost basis of shares distributed and capital gains tax treatment on the NUA. To be considered a "lump-sum payment," the distribution would need to be the entire vested balance to the credit of the participant in the plan. That would include the participant's balance in the ESOP component and the 401(k) component.
- *Forfeitures.* A forfeiture of a nonvested balance may only occur upon a complete distribution of the plan benefit or after five breaks in service. If the vested 401(k) account is distributed to a terminated participant, but the ESOP account is not distributed until a future year, a complete distribution has not occurred, and the nonvested 401(k) account cannot be forfeited until the earlier of five breaks in service or payment of the vested ESOP benefit.

Communication Challenges

Whether a plan sponsor is introducing a second plan or a KSOP, communication challenges await. It is helpful to develop a "Plan Highlights" summary that describes each plan and its objectives. It may also be helpful to draft FAQs (frequently asked questions) for each plan. If the second plan is an ESOP or KSOP, a communication rollout and continuing communication program are often beneficial. Many companies establish a committee that is tasked with the challenge of explaining the benefit programs to participants, answering questions, and providing updates. Be prepared to answer:

- Why did the company adopt this plan?
- Who benefits from the plan? How do I benefit?
- How does it work?
- When do I get a statement?
- When do I get my money?
- With respect to the ESOP:
  - What is an ESOP? Do other companies have an ESOP? Who?
  - What is "beneficial ownership" of employer stock? What does employee ownership mean?
  - Who determines the price of a share of stock?
  - How do I get shares?
  - What makes the share price change?
  - Why do I have to wait so long for the distribution of my account? I can get my 401(k) money right away when I terminate employment.
  - Why are the company's plans so different from each other?

Also, it is important to remember that stock ownership itself does not drive employee performance. Employees act more like owners when they understand what determines a company's success and profitability and how their ideas, attitudes, and work habits can affect a company's performance. In turn, they need to understand how the company's success benefits them as employee-owners. Many successful ESOP companies understand that their employees need to know how their business makes money, handles competitive challenges, and innovates to meet technological and other challenges. Employee-owners also want to know how their companies are performing. Communication programs are ongoing. Successful ESOP companies are often the ones that provide continuous updates on company performance.

Conclusion

To establish and maintain an ESOP and a 401(k) plan, or a KSOP, a great deal of time and energy is required to design the plan(s) and to keep them compliant. Having experts to guide you through administrative and legal issues is a must. But the time and energy are worth it if the benefit is valued by employees and aids the company in recruitment and employee loyalty.

APPENDIX A

ERISA Section 408(b)(2) Vendor Fee Disclosure Rules

In February 2012, the DOL released final ERISA Section 408(b)(2) rules governing fee disclosure by service providers.[1] July 1, 2012, was the deadline for "covered service providers" (CSPs) to disclose fee information to plan sponsors. Under the rules, a CSP is a service provider that enters into a contract or arrangement with a covered plan and that reasonably expects to receive at least $1,000 in total direct *and* indirect compensation during a contract term for providing certain services. The threshold applies if $1,000 or more is paid to a service provider, its affiliates, or subcontractors.

Services covered by the rules include:

1. Services as a fiduciary or registered investment advisor
   a. A fiduciary service provider or registered investment advisor providing services directly to the plan.
   b. A fiduciary providing services to an investment contract, product, or entity that holds plan assets in which the covered plan has an equity interest.

---

1. 77 Fed. Reg. 5,632 (Feb. 3, 2012), codified at 29 CFR § 2550.408b-2(c).

   c. Investment advice provided directly to the covered plan by a registered investment advisor under either the Investment Advisors Act of 1940 or state law.

2. Recordkeepers or brokers providing service to participant-directed plans if one or more investment alternatives are made available through an arrangement connected to the recordkeeper or broker.
3. Other services rendered in exchange for indirect compensation (including third-party administration services if the TPA reasonably expects to receive indirect compensation).

"Direct compensation" includes:

1. Direct payments out of a plan account.
2. Charges to a forfeiture account in a plan, or an ERISA recapture account in a plan.
3. Direct charges to an individual participant's accounts.
4. Plan reimbursements to a company for expenses it paid on a plan's behalf.

"Indirect compensation" includes, for example, compensation received for services rendered to a plan from sources *other than* directly from the plan or plan sponsor. This could include such items as 12b-1 fees collected by a broker/dealer or shareholder service fees paid by a mutual fund company to a TPA, finder's fees, commissions, incentive compensation based on business place, or other soft-dollar arrangements.

> ***Example 1.*** TPA for ABC Company 401(k) and Employee Stock Ownership Plan (KSOP) invoices the plan sponsor directly for annual plan administration services. In addition, TPA receives revenue sharing from American Funds as the daily recordkeeper for the participant-directed portion of the KSOP. Receipt of indirect compensation makes the TPA a CSP if total direct and indirect compensation over the life of the arrangement equals $1,000 or more.

Example 2. A broker for ABC Company receives commissions and 12b-1 fees for services connected to the purchase, sale, or continued monitoring of mutual funds held by an ESOP. The broker is likely a CSP.

What Does This Mean for an ESOP (or KSOP) Sponsor?

The plan sponsor needs to determine what parties are potential CSPs and which CSPs may be receiving direct and indirect compensation for plan services. The plan sponsor should verify that it has written agreements or contracts that outline services to be provided. The plan sponsor may wish to request that these agreements state in writing whether the service provider, an affiliate, or a subcontractor is a fiduciary.

The CSP must disclose in writing to a responsible plan fiduciary the payment arrangement, the party paying it indirect compensation, and the services being provided in exchange for the compensation it is receiving. Disclosures are required before the fiduciary agrees to hire the provider or extend its contract. For existing contracts, the initial disclosure needed to be made before the July 1, 2012, effective date (or before inception of the contract if later). Thereafter, CSPs must make required disclosures before extending, renewing, or modifying contracts. CSPs must also disclose the manner of payment—whether fees are to be billed to the plan or sponsor, deducted from plan accounts, charged against plan investments, etc. Also, there is a requirement to disclose compensation that a CSP reasonably expects to receive in connection with contract termination. A CSP must also disclose whether it or an affiliate or subcontractor will provide any services to the plan as a fiduciary.

There are a number of disclosures that apply specifically to brokers, investment advisors, and certain plan fiduciaries. While those requirements might not apply to an independent TPA who is not acting as a custodian or in any fiduciary capacity, it is important to remember that a TPA who is receiving indirect compensation will come under the disclosure requirements of ERISA Section 408(b)(2).

APPENDIX B

ERISA Section 404(a)(5) Participant Fee Disclosure Rules

Participant-directed accounts within a Section 401(k) plan come under the fee disclosure rules of ERISA Section 404(a) that were released on October 20, 2010,[1] but whose effective dates were later delayed somewhat.[2] The daily recordkeepers for 401(k), profit-sharing, or other plans with self-directed investments have been primarily responsible for preparing either a draft or final version of the annual disclosure notice. Additionally, quarterly disclosures to participants may also apply.

Whether an ESOP, or the ESOP portion of a KSOP, comes under the participant fee disclosure rules depends on whether the ESOP provides for any participant-directed investment. Examples of plans that would fall under these rules would include:

- An ESOP that provides for diversification rights *within* the ESOP; that is, the ESOP provides that participants who attain the age of 55

1. 75 Fed. Reg. 64,910 (Oct. 20, 2010), codified at 29 CFR § 2550.404a-5.
2. For calendar-year plans, the deadline for delivery of the first annual disclosure notices under ERISA Section 404(a) was August 30, 2012. For fiscal year plans, the deadline was the later of (1) 60 days after the first day of the plan year beginning on or after November 1, 2011, or (2) August 30, 2012. 76 Fed. Reg. 42,539 (July 19, 2011).

and complete 10 years of plan participation may diversify a portion of their employer stock accounts and invest funds from liquidated shares within three or more alternative investment funds within the ESOP. Participants eligible to diversify investment would be entitled to participant fee disclosure notices.

- An ESOP provides for reshuffling of the shares allocated to the accounts of participants who have terminated employment. According to a stated formula in the ESOP document, shares allocated to terminated participant accounts are replaced with cash, and participants are offered the right to self-direct investment of that cash. Participants who could self-direct investment would be entitled to participant fee disclosure information as required by ERISA Section 404(a)(5).
- An ESOP provides for diversification *only* by means of a transfer to the company's 401(k) plan. By restricting diversification rights (there is no distribution option), the employer stock in the ESOP becomes a de facto "designated investment alternative" that must be considered when completing a required participant fee disclosure notice that would accompany diversification election forms.
- An ESOP provides participants with two diversification options: distribution or transfer to the company's 401(k) plan. Some believe that a literal reading of Section 404(a)(5) would require participant fee disclosures.
- A KSOP provides for participant-directed investment in the 401(k) portion of the plan. Additionally, participant ESOP accounts may be charged for distribution processing fees and the costs of an annual stock appraisal. In this case, the annual participant fee disclosure notice for participants should include the "standard" 401(k) disclosures, plus information about any fees that might be charged against ESOP accounts.

If an ESOP provides for participant-directed investment, the plan sponsor should become familiar with the overall disclosure rules and determine what parties will provide annual disclosures, quarterly disclosures, and other information to participants on request.

Items to Be Included in Initial and Annual Disclosures

Required Plan Information

General Information

- Current list of investment options
- Explanation of how individuals may give investment instructions
- If applicable, a description of any brokerage window or similar arrangement

Administrative and variable expense information

- Explanation of any expenses that may be deducted from accounts for plan administration—recordkeeping, accounting, legal, or other fees
- Explanation of any fees charged specifically to an individual's account based on participant actions (e.g., loan fees, distribution fees, or QDRO processing fees)

Required Investment Information

Investments that do not have a fixed rate of return

- One-, 5-, and 10-year returns for investments
- The name and returns of the appropriate broad-based securities market index over the related 1-, 5-, and 10-year periods
- Total annual operating expenses expressed as a percentage of assets and as a dollar amount for each $1,000 invested; any shareholder-type fees or restrictions on a participant's ability to purchase or withdraw from the investment (commissions, sales loads, redemption fees, etc.)

Investments that do have a fixed rate of return

- Annual rate of return and term of the investment
- Any shareholder type fees or restrictions on a participant's ability to purchase or withdraw from the investment

Annuity options

- Name of contract, fund, or product; the option's objectives or goals; the benefits and factors that determine price
- Any limitations on the ability of a participant or beneficiary to withdraw or transfer amounts and fees related to transfers or withdrawals
- A statement that insurance company guarantees are subject to its long-term financial strength and claims-paying ability

Other investment information

- A website address through which participants and beneficiaries can obtain additional information about the plan's investment options
- A glossary of terms to assist participants and beneficiaries in understanding the plan's investment options, or a website that provides the glossary

Note that additional disclosures may be required for any target date or similar funds.

Quarterly Disclosures

The statement must contain the dollar amount of any plan-related fees and expenses (administrative expenses or variable fees such as distribution or loan fees) charged to or deducted from an individual's account, along with a description of the services provided for the fees. If applicable, provide an explanation that some of the expenses were paid out of revenue sharing or similar monies connected to the fund options. Calendar-year plans had to furnish the first quarterly disclosure by November 14, 2012. Generally, the quarterly disclosures are due within 45 days after the end of a quarter.

Information on Request

Information to be provided on request from a participant or beneficiary includes:

- A prospectus or SEC-approved summary
- Copies of any financial statements, reports, or similar materials pertaining to investment options, to the extent such materials are provided to the plan
- A statement of the value of a share or unit of a designated investment alternative, along with the date of valuation
- A list of assets that comprise the portfolio of each designated investment alternative, and the value of such assets or the proportion of the investment that it comprises

Disclosures under ERISA Section 404(a) can be combined with other disclosure materials. Electronic fee disclosure rules are available for consideration. The DOL has provided an alternative to its general e-delivery rules, as explained in its Technical Release 2011-03R.

It is possible to handle the annual disclosure through a single communication or through a series of communications. The DOL has a model chart to show how investment disclosures could be communicated.

Action Items for Affected ESOPs or KSOPs

Review the fee disclosure rules and determine who will be responsible for the initial and annual disclosures, and who will be responsible for investment-related disclosures. Then, determine whether quarterly disclosures will apply and who will address the disclosure requirements if they apply.

This appendix covers some of the basic fee disclosure considerations for an ESOP or KSOP, but it does not explain all the nuances of ERISA Section 404(a)(5).

About the Authors

Lisa A. Durham is of counsel with the law firm Krieg DeVault LLP in its Indianapolis office. She has expertise in a wide range of retirement plan matters (e.g., ESOPs, 401(k) plans, profit sharing plans, money purchase plans, 403(b) plans, 457 plans, and stock plans), including the correction of ESOP and other plan failures and prohibited transactions under the IRS and DOL correction programs. Lisa has experience in ESOP and KSOP plan design, stock purchase/sale transactions, ESOP loans, repurchase liability, fiduciary education, plan testing, and DOL and IRS audits.

Dawn Hafner is an assistant vice president for strategic business solutions at VOYA. Dawn has over 20 years of experience in the qualified plan area, including with ESOPs. Her experience has been focused on consulting, compliance, and plan document issues. She has earned the American Society of Pension Actuaries designations of CPC (Certified Pension Consultant) and QPA (Qualified Plan Administrator). Dawn frequently speaks at ESOP conferences and has taught many full-day CPE seminars for various state CPA societies.

Dolores Lawrence is a senior vice president of plan administration at Blue Ridge Associates. She is a CPA, holds the QKA designation from the American Society of Pension Professionals and Actuaries

(ASPPA), and has 30 years of experience in plan design, administration, and consulting services for ESOPs and 401(k) plans. She is a member of the NCEO, the ESOP Association, and ASPPA, and is a speaker at various ESOP conferences.

About the NCEO

The National Center for Employee Ownership (NCEO) is a nonprofit organization that has supported the employee ownership community since 1981. Our mission is to help employee ownership thrive. We have more than 3,000 members because we help people make smart decisions about employee ownership, with everything from reliable information on technical issues to helping companies reach the full potential of employee ownership.

We generate original research, facilitate the exchange of best practices at our live and online events, feature the best and most current writing by experts in our publications, and help employee ownership companies build ownership cultures where employees think and act like owners.

Membership Benefits

NCEO members receive the following benefits and more:

- Customizable communication materials
- Weekly live webinars presented by experts in the field, plus recordings of past webinars
- Peer networking groups where members join in facilitated discussions about communications, finance, HR, and more

- Leadership cohorts that gather CEOs and leaders from select industries
- The *Employee Ownership Report,* with new and up-to-the-minute articles and resources
- Resource-rich curated toolkits
- Personalized support for your employee ownership questions
- Sample documents and checklists from trusted sources
- Actionable data from our research team
- Captive insurance group eligibility and other benefits from affiliated groups
- Preferential prices on all paid resources

To join as a member or order publications, visit our website at www.nceo.org. Visit us at www.nceo.org/r/401 to order this book.

Made in the USA
Monee, IL
04 November 2026

67376113R00036